Evansville—Then & Now ©1995 by Scripps Howard Publishing, Inc. All rights reserved. Printed in the United States of America. No part of this book may be used or reproduced in any manner whatsoever without written permission except in the case of reprints in the context of reviews. For information, write Scripps Howard Publishing, Inc. 458 Old State Road, Gibsonia, Pa. 15044, or The Evansville Courier, 300 E. Walnut Street, Evansville, IN 47713, or call 812-424-7711.

ISBN: 1-884850-06-5

Library of Congress Catalog Card Number: 95-77135

This book documents some of the change that has occurred in Evansville's fascinating history. To do this, we first tracked down old black-and-white photographs of prominent or interesting locations. Some of these pictures dated back 100 years or more; the most recent was made in 1963. Then, we returned to those locations to shoot new color photographs from the exact spot the original picture was made. In some instances, the original view was obscured by trees or buildings that have sprouted in the interim. In those cases, the angle of the new picture may differ slightly from the old. Though this book reaches into Evansville's past, its purpose is not to provide a definitive history of the city. We believe you'll find the photographs published here to be interesting and, perhaps, enlightening.

Photographed By Steve Mellon

Text By Donald E. Baker

THE EVANSVILLE COURIER

Edited & Designed by
J. BRUCE BAUMANN

COPYRIGHT © 1995
SCRIPPS HOWARD PUBLISHING, INC.
ALL RIGHTS RESERVED

A city and a river

"I had to take Franklin to view the Ohio River from Water Street (I do believe they have changed the name to Riverside Drive, since New York has one) for I could not rest until he had seen one of the most striking American river scenes of which I know anything. ... (T)his sweep of the Ohio, coming up from the South and turning immediately south again in a mighty elbow which pushes at the low hill on which the city stands, is tremendous. You know this is a mighty river, bearing the muddy waters of half a continent, by merely looking at it. It speaks for itself."

On a 1915 visit to the town where he had spent the happiest years of his adolescence, the eminent American novelist Theodore Dreiser felt compelled to take his friend, illustrator Franklin Booth, to the riverfront. Evansville residents, expatriates and visitors seem inexorably drawn to that place, the place where the city began.

In the pioneer era unbroken forest covered the trans-Allegheny West and forced transportation onto the inland waterways. By 1800 the region's aspiring cities all were located on the great rivers — Pittsburgh, Cincinnati, St. Louis, New Orleans, Louisville, Ky. But growth was hampered by an elemental fact of nature. It was very easy to move cargoes downstream; it was very difficult to fight the current and bring other cargoes back up river.

The first steamboat on the inland rivers journeyed from Pittsburgh to New Orleans in late 1811. One old settler later recalled, "Everybody was on the lookout for the wonderful steamer. Finally she appeared, waking the silence of the forest with her voice, and attracting to the riverside all the inhabitants along the shore."

Though it was small and primitive compared to the later floating palaces, that steamboat heralded a transportation revolution. With power exponentially greater than what could be forced from muscle or coaxed from sail, it could move people and merchandise almost as easily upstream as down.

The steamboat awakened not only the silence but also the nascent capitalism of those inhabitants along the shore. This new industry would seem to guarantee wealth to people farsighted enough to acquire likely townsites on navigable waterways. One of the many individuals who made his way to the federal land office at Vincennes after the spring thaw of 1812 was Hugh McGary Jr. On terms of $2 per acre with four years to pay, McGary on March 27, 1812, purchased just shy of 441 acres on a horseshoe bend of the Ohio River.

McGary's tract lay at the "one o'clock" position of the great bend. It was roughly bounded by present-day Fulton Avenue north to Lloyd Expressway, then east to Baker Avenue, then south along a line that becomes Parrett Street, and finally west along the line of Washington Avenue to the riverbank. The site was located upon a bluff, which McGary thought was high above all possible flood. Unfortunately he has been proved wrong on a half dozen or so occasions, most notably in 1937 when 500 city blocks of Evansville were under water.

At the same time, other entrepreneurs were platting other towns — Newburgh, for example. McGary needed all the advantages he could get to encourage prospective purchasers to buy their town lots from him rather than from someone else, somewhere else.

One advantage would be to have his new town designated the "permanent" seat of government of a county. With the help of a Gibson County legislator, Robert M. Evans, a new county, named Warrick after a militiaman killed at the Battle of Tippecanoe, was created in 1813. It stretched long and low beside the Ohio from the Harrison County line to the mouth of the Wabash River, and its county seat would be the town McGary had named Evansville after the helpful legislator.

Unfortunately, the Indiana General Assembly soon shattered McGary's and Evansville's prospects when it created Posey County, with Pigeon Creek as its eastern boundary. Warrick County government departed Evansville for the more centrally located, but now defunct, town of Darlington.

McGary found himself with a "cash flow problem," which was alleviated when Evans and his brother-in-law, James W. Jones, purchased a one-third interest in the town-founding enterprise. They devised a new town plat on about 200 acres of McGary's original land, with streets running parallel to the river from northwest to southeast.

Evansville was incorporated in 1817 and again became a county seat when Vanderburgh County was organized on Jan. 7, 1818. The county was named for Henry Vanderburgh, a deceased chief judge of the Indiana territorial supreme court. A newspaper advertisement in April 1818 touted Evansville's future "as a place of landing and deposit for the western part of the State of Indiana" which "certainly holds out a fairer prospect to become a considerable commercial town, than any other in the western part of the state. Merchants, mechanics and men of enterprise are particularly invited to come and judge for themselves."

The town grew surely but it grew slowly. Its economic take-off point did not come until the early 1830s when Indiana unveiled plans to build the longest canal in the world, a 400-mile ditch connecting the Great Lakes at Toledo, Ohio, with the inland rivers at Evansville.

The canal would not only open up the interior of Indiana to commerce, but also it would create an inland transportation route from New Orleans to New York City via the Mississippi and Ohio rivers, this new Wabash and Erie Canal, Lake Erie, New York state's Erie Canal and the Hudson River. No wonder the old county histories record that the city fathers got rip-roaring drunk in the streets when the project was announced.

Evansville seemed destined to become "The Crossroads of America," a distinction that another Indiana city would later claim. "Merchants, mechanics and men of enterprise" came flooding in. Fortunately they did not then know, as people have learned since, that Indiana transportation projects often take 20 years to build and are obsolete when completed. Such was the case with the canal. Its construction bankrupted the state. It was so poorly engineered that it would not hold water, unlike modern expressways that hold water very efficiently. By the time the Wabash and Erie was finished in 1853, plans were already being made to build railroads parallel to its route.

Ironically, when the canal was completed it did not terminate in Evansville at all. By 1837, a tract of land astraddle Pigeon Creek had come into the hands of four developers, two named Law, one named Macoll and one named Scott. Scrunching their names together they came up with "Lamasco" as the name of the new town they platted from First Avenue westward to St. Joseph Avenue. Unlike Evansville, Lamasco's streets were laid out on the cardinal points, due north-south and east-west.

By the 1850s, Lamasco had annexed land up to the Evansville corporate limits and was threatening to landlock its rival by annexing more ground east of First Avenue. Had this situation continued it would have resulted in a permanent competition for growth, but at the urging of the leaders of both towns, the Indiana legislature authorized a merger in 1857. By referendum the citizens of the new combined city voted to continue the name Evansville. Lamasco disappeared from the map, but its street grid did not. It eventually surrounded the original "cockeyed" McGary-Evans-Jones grid. Thus, anyone entering or leaving downtown

Evansville finds that the street eventually makes a confusing oblique-angle turn in one direction or another.

Many businesses set up shop in Evansville during those early decades, including The Evansville Courier which printed its "volume 1, number 1" in 1845. But the era of Evansville's greatest growth was the second half of the 19th century, following the disruptions of the Civil War. The steamboat trade was at its height. Evansville was a major stop for through boats in Pittsburgh-New Orleans commerce, and it was the home port for a number of steamboat companies engaged in local and regional or "packet" trade. In 1870 the city added substantially to its area and population when it annexed the West Side, or, as some would have it, the "Best Side."

Three of Evansville's most beloved buildings — the Old Post Office from the 1870s, Willard Library from the 1880s, and the Old Courthouse from the 1890s — are monuments to those decades when factory whistles screeched morning, noon and night, and steamboats lined up six deep to take on Evansville products for the world's markets.

Evansville was positioned geographically for commerce, and, thanks to an abundance of rich nearby natural resources, it had something to sell. Dreiser described the riverfront in the early 1880s, viewed "from the end of Main Street, which debouched upon an enormous sloping levee, paved with great grey cobblestones and stocked with enormous piles of cotton in bales, groceries and hardware in boxes, and watermelons and other fruits and vegetables in piles or crated, boxed, bagged or barreled. Among these were little artificial streets or lanes, along which traveled constantly scores of small mule-drawn drays driven by Negroes in sleeveless cotton undershirts and belted trousers gripped tightly about the hips.

"At the foot of the levee, where it met the water, were long, brown wharves or floating docks, anchored lengthwise of the shore, and lashed to those again, a number of the old-time, stern wheel river steamers, with their black double stacks, double and treble decks, gilt and red or blue or green decorations, and piles of freight being taken on or unloaded."

The products of the fertile farmland surrounding the city found their way to those wharves and were the basis for a growing flour and corn milling industry.

Coal mines began operating literally on Evansville's doorstep in the 1850s with the digging of the Ingleside Mine on Coal Mine (now Reitz) Hill. By the turn of the century there were 10 mine shafts within or near the city limits. Those mines provided fuel for industry, steamboats and railroad locomotives, and for commercial and household heating. Evansville flourished under a cloud of coal smoke and soot.

Foundries served the mechanical needs of the steamboats and branched out into the manufacture of farm implements and household stoves.

Hardwood lumber, rafted down the Green River from the heart of Western Kentucky, fed a large-scale lumber and furniture industry, the sawmills and factories for which lined Pigeon Creek after 1870. By 1900, Evansville was one of the largest hardwood furniture centers in the world, with 41 factories employing approximately 2,000 workers.

Fortunes made in mining, manufacturing, and, particularly, the wholesale trade found an outlet in the construction of the imposing Victorian-era homes that have become an attraction for tourists and "gentrifiers" in the Riverside Drive and First Street area.

By this time the character of the city had been

fixed and its main ethnic groups were in place — the original Protestant Scotch-Irish from the upland South, Catholic Irish come for canal or railroad work, a smattering of sharp New York and Vermont businessmen, Germans fleeing Europe for religious, economic or military reasons, and newly freed former slaves from Western Kentucky, swelling the small prewar free black population.

Evansville, as Dreiser described it, was a civic trinity, three cities in one: It "is a southern city, in spite of the fact that it is Indiana, and has all the characteristic marks of a southern city — a hot, drowsy, almost enervating summer, an early spring, a mild winter, a long, agreeable autumn. Snow falls but rarely and does not endure long."

Negroes "are about, whole sections of them, and work on the levee, the railroad, and at scores of tasks given over to whites in the north. — It is as though the extreme south had reached up and just touched this projecting section of Indiana." For nearly a century, southern attitudes would make Evansville a segregated city.

"Again," says Dreiser, "it is a German city, strangely enough, a city to which thousands of the best type of German have migrated. ... (H)ere in Evansville German names abounded. ... There are a number of purely German Catholic or Lutheran churches controlled by Bavarian priests or ministers.

"Again it is a distinctly river type of town, with that floating population of river squatters — you can always tell them — drifting about ... river nomads or gypsies bustling about, dark, sallow, small, rugged."

Despite being a "river type of town," Evansville was no longer so dependent upon the steamboats. The city became an important node in the nation's railroad network in 1887 when the Louisville and Nashville Railroad constructed a bridge across the Ohio River and a major rail yard southwest of Evansville, with the new town of Howell created to house railroad employees. In 1916 Evansville would annex Howell, completing the city's counterclockwise march around the horseshoe bend.

Beginning in the 1890s, Evansville was also the center of a sprawling interurban transportation system. Oversized streetcars powered by overhead electric wires provided frequent and convenient freight and passenger service north as far as Patoka, Ind., west to Mount Vernon, Ind., east to Rockport, Ind., and south, via ferry, to Henderson, Ky. These "traction lines," which today's urban transportation planners would call "light rail," lasted some four decades until they were replaced by buses in the 1930s.

Change in Evansville's economic base continued as a new century began. Workers gradually shifted from making furniture and stoves to assembling cars and refrigerators. Chrysler began making Plymouths on the city's north side in 1934, while nearby Seeger, Sunbeam, and Servel churned out replacements for the country's iceboxes.

In the 1920s, while jazz blared, skirts went up and booze went out, the Ku Klux Klan came in, offering people an outlet for their outrage at an apparent loss of American patriotism, white supremacy, Protestant ethics, and family values. From a small seed planted in Evansville, the Indiana Klan grew in less than half a decade to briefly take over not only the city government but also the state government.

Despite social unrest, in the decades of the 1920s and 1930s city leaders attempted to improve Evansville's transportation position. As the federal highway system developed, Evansville managed to have itself located on the Chicago-to-

Miami "Dixie Bee Highway," later U.S. Highway 41. The city's favorable location on north-south trade routes was solidified by the construction of a highway bridge across the Ohio River in 1932. The city also took its first steps in airport development in the 1930s.

The Great Depression of the 1930s was a time of high unemployment and business and banking failure, notwithstanding the timely arrival of Chrysler. Perversely, the 1937 flood proved to be of a morale booster by showing that the city could pull together to confront a major crisis. With the steamboats gone, it also resulted in Evansville's turning its back on the Ohio. To keep the river out of the residents' yards and basements, the city joined with the federal government in a half century of levee construction that penned and hid the Ohio behind a barrier of earthen berms and concrete walls.

The discovery of oil in the area on the eve of World War II made Evansville something of a boom town, complete with high-stakes gambling dens (and a thoroughbred racetrack) on the orphaned piece of Kentucky north of the river. The war itself, and the attendant rapid growth of industry, finally wiped away the last lingering effects of the Depression. For the duration, the Plymouth factory was converted into an ordnance plant which turned out "billions of bullets," and other companies switched over to the manufacture of war materiel.

In 1942 the city acquired a factory adjacent to the airport north of the city for the manufacture of P-47 Thunderbolt fighter aircraft and a huge shipyard complex on the riverfront east of St. Joseph Avenue for the construction of oceangoing LSTs (Landing Ship-Tanks). Employment jumped from 21,000 to 64,000 in just a few months. The city's population grew as newcomers from throughout the Tri-State arrived to take advantage of the new employment opportunities.

What with the city bursting with war workers, Navy crews waiting to pick up their LSTs, dashing test pilots fresh from the cockpits of their Thunderbolts and soldiers on weekend passes from training at Camp Breckinridge just across the river, Evansville was a jumping place on Saturday nights.

After the war the shipyard and aircraft plant closed, but employment continued to climb as consumers could at last purchase goods unavailable during the war. There was a great national clamor for automobiles, household appliances and farm equipment, Evansville's bread-and-butter industries. Pent-up housing demand caused residential development to leap north across Pigeon Creek and east across Weinbach Avenue, the pre-war limits of urbanization. Men were home from the war, women were home from "temporary" wartime jobs and the baby boom was on.

By the late 1950s, the existence of this new population, far removed from the traditional downtown commercial area, would encourage the growth of large shopping centers such as North Park on outer First Avenue, Lawndale on Green River Road and, in 1962, Indiana's first covered shopping mall, Washington Square. All shopping roads would no longer lead downtown.

Well-meaning city leaders attempted to hold back the future by using all the urban development tools offered by a generous federal government. Programs of "urban renewal" tore down whole neighborhoods, including the former "red light" district. The area was intersected by First and Second streets, Third Avenue, and High Street and was therefore, perhaps inevitably, referred to as the "gearshift district" or "Geartown."

Next, urban renewal leveled the old steamboat warehouse district between Second Street and the Ohio, an area of multistory brick and terra cotta buildings erected in the prosperous glory days of the steamboat trade. In a brick-and-mortar feeding frenzy, the wrecking cranes also gobbled up a

smorgasbord of prominent landmarks, including Assumption Cathedral, old Central High School, the Chicago and Eastern Illinois Railroad Depot-cum-Community Center, and every downtown theater except the Victory.

In just one half decade from 1958 to 1963 nearly $30 million was spent on urban renewal. This spending reached its peak with the completion of the $25 million Civic Center Complex, on the previous site of the 100-year-old Cook's Brewery and several city blocks' worth of buildings, in 1968.

The city fathers also attempted to lure shoppers back downtown by reconstructing Main Street into an imitation shopping center and allowing people to walk in the roadway, but to no avail. In subsequent decades the development of Green River Road from shopping center to bigger-and-brighter shopping center would make that old country road Evansville's new commercial "Main Street."

Meanwhile, with the end of the Korean War came nationwide recession. Because of heavy dependence on two durable goods industries with close ties to defense contractors, the downturn was particularly severe in Evansville. Servel went out of business, Chrysler terminated its local operations and other businesses disappeared as well.

The Evansville economy was saved from total collapse by the 28 businesses that moved into the area between 1955 and 1963. Whirlpool was one of those, as were Alcoa and General Electric.

Today the retail and wholesale trade upon which the city was founded continues to expand, but service providers have become even more important. The health service industry is Evansville's largest employer, and the city has become the major provider of health-care services in the Tri-State. The payroll represented by education, including a large public school system, the University of Evansville, the University of Southern Indiana and Ivy Tech is also significant.

From small beginnings before World War II, Evansville has become a major plastics production center. More than 20 plastics and plastics-related companies employing over 6,000 people are located in or near Evansville.

But, as The Evansville Courier passes its 150th year, and Evansville its 183rd, the wheel of history has returned to its point of origin. Once again we look to the Ohio and to a riverboat to provide economic sustenance. Some people believe, and many other people hope, that the *City of Evansville*, Aztar Corporation's floating gambling casino, will fulfill its promise of economic benefits and riverfront revitalization.

It is well to remember, however, that there was once another riverboat, "the very embodiment of beauty, grace, and elegance," that "came gallantly to the wharf" on March 7, 1870, "amid the waving of handkerchiefs and the most enthusiastic cheers of the populace." "We the people of Evansville," the city's reigning orator assured the boat's owners, "feel grateful for your enterprise and liberality in having brought within our waters this, the pride of our people. It is but another evidence of our increasing prosperity and greatness."

Unfortunately, that vessel had only an eight-month career. During the night of November 21, 1870, Evansville's dreams went up in the smoke of a great fire. The conflagration destroyed not only the new boat but also two other steamboats and the Evansville wharfboat, the floating warehouse to which all three were tied. The city's economy was worse off than before the boat arrived.

That ill-fated riverboat, too, was named the *City of Evansville*.

— ***Donald E. Baker***

EVANSVILLE
Then & Now

SPECIAL COLLECTIONS, WILLARD LIBRARY OF EVANSVILLE

The older of these two photographs is entitled "Birdseye View from Courthouse," in the 1901 published album of Evansville scenes, "Artwork of Evansville." One of the most popular Evansville photos used for decorating the walls of local offices and fast-food restaurants, it illustrates the profound changes that nearly a century of flood, fire, urban "renewal" and "Downtown revitalization" have wrought.

Of the buildings shown in the older photo, the only ones also present in the modern picture are the Old Sheriff's Residence and Jail in the center foreground and the Old Post Office in the upper left background.

Other prominent buildings in the older photo include the German Methodist Church at lower left and Holy Trinity Roman Catholic Church in the center, with its school to its left. Both congregations were made up of German-speaking first- and second-generation immigrants. The German Methodist Church building, minus its steeple, was later used as the Vanderburgh County Health Department. Holy Trinity Church was struck by lightning and burned the night of April 2, 1950, and was replaced by the modern, one-story Pro-Cathedral of the Most Holy Trinity.

The Old Jail was built at the same time as the Old Courthouse, and the two were connected by a tunnel under Fourth Street to facilitate the transit of prisoners. It was designed as a scaled-down

_C. 1900_

German castle in order, it is said, to instill the proper respect for authority in the newly arrived Germans. The last Vanderburgh County sheriff to live with his family in the residence portion of the Old Jail was Sheriff Jerry Riney.

The large buildings behind the Old Post Office, convenient to the steamboat landing, were erected after the Civil War to house Evansville's thriving wholesale businesses. They were razed in the early 1970s when Landeco, an out-of-town development firm, presented elaborate plans to replace the entire decaying warehouse district with a grand complex of hotels, offices and apartments. The Riverside One apartment building, the multi-story building at center-right in the modern photograph, was the only part of the plan realized before Landeco went bankrupt.

The remainder of the cleared land lay fallow for nearly two decades before local developers began building various structures piecemeal, without the coordination of a Landeco-like unified vision.

In the very bottom center can be seen three of the 14 allegorical sculptures that are present on the gutterline of the four facades of the Old Courthouse. Only one of the 14 figures is male. The rest are women, some of them in states of bare-breastedness that apparently did not shock our Victorian ancestors but would likely meet with vocal disapproval by critics of public art if a modern sculptor attempted to put them on a government building today.

C. 1995

11

SPECIAL COLLECTIONS, WILLARD LIBRARY OF EVANSVILLE

Willard Library and Park were projected in 1876 by Willard Carpenter, an Evansville dry goods merchant, failed railroad builder and land speculator. It replaced Carpenter's earlier dream of founding a college. The library was to be both a circulating and reference library "for the use of the people of all classes, races and sexes, free of charge forever." That was a very liberal idea at a time when many "libraries" were private-association reading rooms for adult white males only.

For twenty-six years Willard was the city's only public library. By the turn of the century, Evansville had spread out so far that there was a movement to establish convenient neighborhood branches. Since Willard's charter and its funds prevented its filling that need, city leaders petitioned Pittsburgh steel magnate Andrew Carnegie, who was providing libraries to hundreds of towns throughout the country, to help set up another library. That request was granted, and since 1911 Evansville has had the distinction of having two public libraries, separately administered, each of which has developed a particular role in the community.

C. 1911

A row of "shotgun" houses already existing on "Carpenter's Field" when the library opened in 1885 were retained for a number of years as a source of rental income. The long, skinny "shotgun," a one-room wide house with the interconnecting doors neatly lined up, was the typical laboring-man's house in Evansville starting in the 1860s.

The scene at left shows the dedication in 1911 of a water fountain for horses in the intersection of First Avenue and Pennsylvania Street. It was one of more than 100 placed in cities across the country by the National Humane Alliance. Although now relegated to farms, racetracks and history books, horses remained part of the Evansville ambience for several years to come. But when at least one automobile showed up for the dedication ceremony, participants might have realized that the future usefulness of this fancy equine watering trough would be limited.

Half a century later the fountain was moved to Main Street as part of the Walkway beautification of the 1970 period. Now, when the stoplights are green, cars whiz unobstructed through the intersection and on under Lloyd Expressway.

C. 1995

SPECIAL COLLECTIONS, WILLARD LIBRARY OF EVANSVILLE

The corner of Main and Fifth streets, one view showing Main Street as it really looked in the "old days" about 1913, and the other showing Main Street after it was rebuilt into a pedestrian mall to look like the "old days" 70 years later. Union Federal Savings Bank, soon to be merged into Citizens National Bank, now occupies that corner and owns all but one of the other properties on that block face.

Real streetcars ran on tracks, powered by overhead electric wires, from the 1890s to the 1930s. The more recent reincarnation of Main Street features small buses cleverly masquerading as trolleys. Bicycles became popular at the end of the 19th century as a convenient mode of travel for

those who did not always have carfare. And, of course, one could always resort to "shank's mare," that is, one's own two feet.

The corner building in 1913 was Martin Emig's Manhattan Cafe. On its roof was a longtime landmark, a sign advertising Evansville-brewed Sterling Beer, with moving lights pouring heady foam into a glass at third-floor level.

Across the street is the William Hughes Department Store building, the last home of one of Evansville's earliest retail companies. Later the location of a J.C. Penney store, the building has been an abandoned pigeon rookery for several years and is, thankfully, obscured by Main Street's ubiquitous Bradford pear trees in the more recent photo.

C. 1995

SPECIAL COLLECTIONS, WILLARD LIBRARY OF EVANSVILLE

Evansville opened its first public schools in loaned church buildings in 1854. The next year operations began in a combination elementary and high school on a site at Fourth and Mulberry streets, now occupied by part of the Welborn Hospital complex.

On Sept. 6, 1868, Evansville High School moved to Seventh Street (now Martin Luther King Blvd.) between Vine and Court streets. "It is," the Evansville Journal reported the next day, "the handsomest and one of the most substantial school buildings in the state, and will for many generations, stand a proud and beautiful monument to the liberality of our citizens towards the cause of education."

Renamed Central High School when Reitz High School opened in 1918, the campus grew with

periodic additions to cover the entire block between Sixth and Seventh streets, with a gymnasium across the street at Sixth and Court streets.

A new Central High School, geographically north of North High School, opened in 1971, after a year's delay due to a construction strike. The city's second major historic preservation effort was aimed at saving at least the old building's distinctive tower. Unlike the previous effort to retain the Old Courthouse, the Central Tower drive was not successful. The entire structure soon met the wrecking ball.

In the picture on the right, a parking lot covers the old Central High School site. The old gymnasium, which was subsequently incorporated into the YMCA, can be seen in the left background. The school is gone but, typically, the stoplights remain.

THE EVANSVILLE COURIER

After the Civic Center complex opened in 1969, the federal government offices moved from the Old Post Office, the county vacated the Old Courthouse and the city officials walked away from the old 1887 City Hall on the corner of Third and Walnut streets.

Behind City Hall on Third Street was the Fire Department headquarters, and, some years later, the Police headquarters was constructed near City Hall on Walnut Street.

By the time the three buildings were abandoned, City Hall had been without

its impressive tower for many years. The clock faces are in the collections of the Evansville Museum of Arts and Science. Just as the wrecking ball was about to swing, it was discovered that a large number of "useless" city records had been abandoned along with the building. Those records were saved by quick work on the part of Dr. Darrel Bigham and other faculty and students of then Indiana State University - Evansville. After several years in the care of the Old Courthouse management, the records were moved to Willard Library's local government archives.

C. 1995

SPECIAL COLLECTIONS, WILLARD LIBRARY OF EVANSVILLE

The photograph at left was taken before the 1960s construction of the 40-acre Civic Center complex and the 1980s construction of the Lloyd Expressway. The photo at right shows the drastic changes such projects can impose on the fabric of a city.

The lower left street intersection in the older picture is Seventh and Vine streets, with Assumption Roman Catholic Cathedral and School on the north side of Seventh Street and Cook's Brewery to the east, between Sycamore and Main streets. One block north, at Eighth and Main streets, is the Chicago and Eastern Illinois Railroad Station, later the Community Center.

In the picture on the right the Winfield K. Denton Federal Building has replaced Assumption Cathedral, and the City-County offices and courts stand where once Cook's "Goldblume" Beer was

C. 1956

brewed. The School Corporation offices occupy the depot site, although Eighth Street at that point is hardly even a memory.

The street grids of Evansville and Lamasco were laid out at nearly 45-degree angles to one another. The old picture shows what happened when the two towns grew together. In the old Evansville plat, Main and Sycamore streets are parallel streets coming northwest from the river.

Where the two grid systems meet north of the brewery, Main Street decides to be a north-south street, while Sycamore Street prefers to become an east-west street. The two parallel streets thereupon turn, cross, and go their separate ways. And we wonder why visitors (and many residents) get confused driving Downtown.

C. 1995

THE EVANSVILLE COURIER

The original designs for the YMCA building at Fourth and Sycamore streets were by James and Merritt Reid, the architects who designed Willard Library, the Grand Theater and other prominent Evansville buildings in the 1880s. As built, the structure reflected enlargements and enhancements by architect Frank J. Schlotter, who had trained in the Reids' offices.

The Y opened in 1891 and used this building until 1914, when it moved to a newer building at Fifth and Vine streets, across the street from the Old Courthouse. After some years' use as offices, the old Y building was torn down in 1928 to make

way for the magnificent art deco "skyscraper" of the Central Union Bank. The new bank did not weather the Great Depression, and what has been renamed the Hulman Building has long housed the principal offices of the Southern Indiana Gas and Electric Company (SIGECO).

Hulman was Terre Haute wholesale grocery heir Tony Hulman Jr., who married Evansville cigar heiress Mary Fendrich in the 1920s. "Richest Boy in Terre Haute Marries the Richest Girl in Evansville," the society columns blared with amazing frankness. The Hulmans acquired extensive property holdings in both towns, as well as the Indianapolis Motor Speedway.

UNIVERSITY OF SOUTHERN INDIANA SPECIAL COLLECTIONS / UNIVERSITY ARCHIVES

Fourth Street is wider between Locust and Chestnut streets than elsewhere along its length because from the mists of time on into the 1950s the street was a farmers' market. The vendors needed the extra room to back their wagons and, later, their trucks up to the curb to sell their produce off the tailgates.

Once there was a markethouse, or at least a covering over the street, but it was torn down in the 1870s as structurally dangerous. Evansville resident William Lavender later remembered that "Saturday was the big day. After the house was torn down, the market was still continued Saturday and Saturday night. For two blocks, wagons, express wagons, and buggies were backed up to the curb on both sides of the street. Stands were placed up to the walk. All kinds of garden truck, fruit, chickens, eggs, butter, lard, meat, and cheese were exhibited for the thrifty housewife to do her bargaining for Sunday dinner. It was a pleasure to watch the jostling, hilarious crowd, with their market baskets and tin buckets for cider, vinegar or buttermilk; and a string of young folks without any baskets, but with a desire for a lark. They would join the parade to see what was to be seen or meet a friend and visit a while."

C. 1887

The successors of those young folks can now be seen doing much the same nonpurchasing activity at the malls on a Friday night.

In the late 19th century many blacks lived near Fourth Street and patronized the Southern Indiana farmers who sold their wares. Meanwhile, the buildings along the market area were occupied by various businesses — pawn shops, tailor and clothing shops, eating places — many of which were run by Jewish families, some of whom lived "over the store." The interplay of cultures made "Big Market" (another market area across First Avenue from Willard Library was "Little Market") a phenomenon sadly missed by older Evansville residents. Modern health regulations and supermarket competition put the open-air market out of business in the 1950s.

Many of the buildings on the south side of Fourth Street are present in both photographs, the earlier of which is from the 1880s. Except for three storefronts on the corner of Fourth and Locust streets, however, the entire block of buildings on the north side of the street has been razed in the interests of an automobile dealership.

The awning of today's popular Real Bread Company bakery and restaurant nearly replicates the awning visible in the earlier photo.

C. 1995

UNIVERSITY OF SOUTHERN INDIANA SPECIAL COLLECTIONS / UNIVERSITY ARCHIVES

Early on, after the establishment of Vanderburgh County in 1818, county business and court sessions were conducted at the waterfront warehouse of Hugh McGary Jr., Evansville's founder. A new brick courthouse was built at Third and Main streets in 1819-20, on the present site of National City Bank.

In 1852 the County Commissioners awarded James Roquet the contract to build a new, columned, Greek-Revival, $14,000 courthouse cater-cornered across Main Street. Willard Carpenter received the contract to provide a privy commodious enough to accommodate the courthouse visitors and workers.

The courthouse was nearly complete when it was destroyed by fire on Christmas Eve, 1855. Construction started over again, and when the building was finally finished in 1857, inflation had increased its cost to $14,300.

County government remained at Third and Main streets until the third courthouse at Fourth and

C. 1887

Vine streets (the present Old Courthouse) opened in 1891. Not long afterward the second courthouse was replaced by the building block that still houses DeJong's and once also housed Schultz's Department Store. The Schultz's store half burned in the 1980s, and a parking lot now occupies that part of the site.

In 1887, when the earlier photo of the courthouse was taken, the German National Bank was across the street. The bank was founded in 1873 by "citizens who have been identified for many years with the business interest of the city," including iron manufacturer Samuel Orr as president and lumberman John A. Reitz as vice president.

A quickprint company now occupies the bank building, the windows of which have been replaced by brick. Like many other Main Street Walkway buildings, it acquired a plastic canopy in the 1970s, as Evansville attempted to give the Downtown a modern shopping center atmosphere.

SPECIAL COLLECTIONS, WILLARD LIBRARY OF EVANSVILLE

A. P. Lahr and H. E. Bacon were partners in a department store at Sixth and Main streets until 1917 when they became competitors. Bacon kept the old location, and Lahr opened a new store at Fourth and Locust streets.

By 1937, Lahr's was out of business and Schear's New York Department Store had moved in. Schear's had started business nearby, on Fourth Street between Locust and Walnut streets in 1906.

Shoppers still spent their money Downtown when

the photo on the left was taken around 1950, but at Schear's, profit wasn't the only consideration. The Downtown Kiwanis Club had an annual project to provide new shoes and stockings to poor children. The children were provided vouchers to be fitted for the new apparel at the store of active Kiwanian Bill Schear.

The Schear's building was flattened into a parking lot during the early 1960s urban renewal. The Hilliard-Lyons Building, originally Citizen's National Bank, is present in both photographs, with its outside fire escape enclosed in the later picture.

SPECIAL COLLECTIONS, WILLARD LIBRARY OF EVANSVILLE

Architects James and Merritt Reid designed many of the important Evansville buildings of the 1880s, including Willard Library, St. Paul's Episcopal Church and this suite of structures that took up most of Sycamore Street between Second and Third streets — the Vendome Hotel, the Grand Theater and the Business Men's Association (later Grein) Building.

All three were constructed circa 1890, and in a special business edition that year The Evansville Courier gushed, "It is such a masterpiece of architectural ability as the erection of edifices like the Vendome, which advertises a city, and

brings it into prominence throughout this country." The 40-room hotel was "first-class in every respect," and included a saloon with a back-alley entrance: "While common and very popular in other cities to have a first-class saloon in an alley, where people desiring privacy can obtain it, yet it is an entirely new venture in this city, and undoubtedly it will be a big success."

Urban renewal of the 1960s and 1970s took all three buildings. Their ornate, romantic, Gay '90s architecture contrasts starkly with the modern utilitarian style of Citizens National Bank and its parking garage, which replaced them in the 1980s. The cars have changed a bit, too.

C. 1995

SPECIAL COLLECTIONS, WILLARD LIBRARY OF EVANSVILLE

A picture from the early 1930s shows strollers in Sunset Park and the riverfront as it appeared just before Evansville's first "urban renewal" project, courtesy of the 1937 flood. The riverfront buildings took the full force and pressure of the flood's weight and current, and several were so weakened structurally that they had to be taken down after the waters receded.

In the center of the photograph is the building originally constructed for the Vickery Brothers wholesale grocery company. By the time of the photo it housed the Keller-Crescent Printing and Engraving Company, the forerunner of the present, relocated, Keller-Crescent advertising company.

To the right is the McCurdy Hotel building, still present in 1995 as the McCurdy Residential Center retirement and nursing home. At the far right is the building which was built in 1910 as the private Gilbert Sanitarium. At the time of

both pictures it was (and is) the home of the Hadi Shrine Temple.

Nestled between the McCurdy and the Shrine in the older photo is the showroom of Robert W. Baskett Motors, the local dealership of the Graham Motor Car. Brothers Joe, Bob and Ray Graham had been involved in truck manufacturing, a glass company and other Evansville industries and ended up in Detroit when their truck business was bought out by Dodge. They in turn bought the nearly bankrupt Paige-Detroit Motor Company and began producing their own car, the Graham-Paige, in 1927. But, as Joe Graham wrote, they thought "Evansville was the capital of the universe." The Grahams were welcomed back to town with speeches and a parade when they announced plans to build an Evansville automobile factory on East Columbia Street. Unfortunately the Evansville factory closed early in the Depression, and the Grahams ceased making cars altogether during World War II.

THE EVANSVILLE COURIER

There had been a passenger railroad depot at Eighth and Main streets since at least 1882, when railroad magnate David Mackey brought the Reid Brothers architects to Evansville to design a terminal for his Evansville and Terre Haute Railroad. That Victorian station was replaced in 1903-05 by this more modern English Baroque structure for the E&TH's successor, the Chicago and Eastern Illinois Railroad.

Just before World war II, after the Louisville and Nashville Railroad took corporate control of the C&EI, passenger train operations were consolidated at the L&N depot on Fulton Avenue. The C&EI depot then briefly housed a Ford sales agency, but in 1943 it opened as a USO (United Service Organizations) Club for white soldiers, with a canteen, lounge, and recreational facilities, including the occasional dance. After the war the Community Center, which had been located in WPA (Works Progress Administration) facilities in the old Crescent Furniture factory at First Avenue and Franklin Street, moved into the old station.

The depot building was torn down in the 1960s to make way for the Civic Center complex, which

C. 1963

included a new Community Center a couple of blocks to the northeast. The Vanderburgh School Corporation offices now occupy the old depot site, although Eighth Street at that location has become a pedestrian plaza with plantings and fountain.

When the depot was razed, its four impressive Green River limestone columns were salvaged and dumped out near the waterworks. A few years later, when Evansville sought an appropriate way to commemorate the 1976 Bicentennial of the United States, the columns were resurrected as the centerpiece of the Four Freedoms Monument on the riverbank. The monument includes 13 steps in honor of the original colonies, 50 stone tablets representing the present states, and the four columns, upon which are carved a statement of four freedoms important to Americans. Those words incised in everlasting stone are not quite the same as the famous Four Freedoms enunciated by President Franklin D. Roosevelt, but they are good freedoms, nonetheless.

The irony that one of Evansville's most important symbols is made up of the remains of one of its demolished architectural treasures has not been lost on the city's historic preservationists.

PHOTOGRAPH COURTESY C. L. SCHLAMP

The Old United States Post Office and Custom House was constructed in 1875-79, during the era of Evansville's wealth and economic power after the Civil War. It was designed by the Architect of the Treasury, William Appleton Potter, and former Evansville postmaster James H. McNeely supervised the construction, which cost nearly $40,000 less than the $300,000 Congressional appropriation. That is, it was a federal construction project that came in under budget, a fact that alone would justify a historic plaque.

The building was hailed as "one of the most imposing edifices in Evansville, and furnishes commodious apartments (to work in, not to live in) for the postmaster, the surveyor of customs, collector of internal revenue, United States court, United States inspectors of steamboats, and all other government officers." Forty years later those offices no longer seemed sufficiently commodious, and the wings on the building were added. The design called for multicolored stone and slate from the same quarries as those of the original building, and the addition was so sensi-

C. 1927

tively realized that many people have no idea the structure as they now know it was built in two stages four decades apart.

The federal offices moved to the Civic Center in 1969, and the General Services Administration padlocked the doors. After years of depredation by squatters, pigeons, and stained-glass-window thieves, the administration of Mayor Russell Lloyd, under the leadership of Mayoral Assistant Randall Shepard, acquired the building and stabilized, weatherproofed and "mothballed" it. It remained a Sleeping Beauty until Prince Charming appeared in the form of Foster Development Company in the 1980s. The Old Post Office was rehabilitated for restaurants, stores and offices. Behind it, on the site of the former wholesale warehouses that had been torn down by urban renewal, was built the Old Post Office Place, an area for retail and office space surrounding a central parking courtyard.

The 1889 History of Vanderburgh County reported, "A Business Men's Association has been formed, its objects being to effect the betterment of the city and its people in every possible way, and by developing its natural resources to earn for Evansville that rank and recognition among the cities of the world which it ought to receive. The association has already done much good by inducing the establishment here of labor-employing enterprises, and by planning for a magnificent opera-house and public building, now in the course of construction, to cost $100,000. — (A)mong its members are about 500 of the most progressive and advanced citizens of the place."

The office building, six stories of stone, brick and terra cotta, opened at Second and Sycamore streets in 1891. The Courier called it a "monument of architectural perfection," and it was the Reid Brothers' crowning architectural achievement in Evansville. By the time it opened they had already moved on to careers on the West Coast, beginning with the design for San Diego's Hotel del Coronado, one of

SPECIAL COLLECTIONS, WILLARD LIBRARY OF EVANSVILLE

the developers of which was Elisha Babcock of Evansville.

The opera-house, better known as the Grand Theater, adjoined the BMA Building on Sycamore Street and shared a lobby entrance with it. It was also a Reid Brothers design, seating 1,700 people, lighted by electricity and having exceptional acoustics. Described by The Courier in 1890 as "the pride of Evansville and the envy of all strangers," in due course it added movies to its offerings of live theater and vaudeville.

The BMA Building had been renamed the "Grein Building" by the time it and the Grand were demolished by urban renewal in the early 1970s. The "Head of Liberty" from over the entrance of the Grand is now in the sculpture garden of the Evansville Museum. Some of the decorative terra cotta from the BMA Building is also in the Museum's collections.

On the former site of some of Evansville's most exquisite architecture is now located a parking garage for Citizens National Bank.

COLLECTION OF THE EVANSVILLE MUSEUM OF ARTS AND SCIENCE

Automobiles and horses still mix in this picture of the Chestnut Street end of the Fourth Street Market area. The flag-bedecked automobile may be part of a parade or motorcade, perhaps as part of the 1920 election campaign.

The Old Courthouse dome and the old Citizens Bank, now Hilliard-Lyons, Building are visible in both photographs, as are, barely, the three storefronts in the distance at Fourth and Locust streets. All else is gone, leveled for the convenience of the successors of those early autos.

Note also the brick street in the earlier photo, which is probably under the asphalt in the later one. In 1889 Main Street became Evansville's first brick-paved street, and Fourth Street fol-

lowed in 1894. One of the men hired for the Fourth Street bricking crew was a young black man just off the train from St. Louis. His name was W.C. Handy, and in his off-time from laying bricks he got his first job as a professional musician, an $8 gig at a barbecue in Henderson, Ky. There he met Elizabeth Price, the girl he later married. Handy went on to become the composer and publisher of many blues songs, including the very popular "St. Louis Blues." Henderson holds an annual music festival in his honor.

The Old National Bank tower is prominent in the modern photograph.

SPECIAL COLLECTIONS, WILLARD LIBRARY OF EVANSVILLE

Around 1910, West Franklin Street bustled with business activity. For many decades the stretch of Franklin Street from Wabash to St. Joseph avenues was second only to Downtown as a commercial district. The streetcar tracks and power poles ran right down the center of the extrawide street, which was one of the major boulevards of the original Lamasco town plat.

The building on the right, the northwest corner of Tenth Avenue and Franklin Street, was the Sherffius Department Store. By the 1920s the building served as the Dreamland Ballroom, and when it burned down in 1957 it was occupied by Jerry's Market on the ground floor, with the West Side Bowling Lanes above. Jerry's relocated into the one-story building that replaced the Sherffius structure and had only recently gone out of business when the picture on the right was taken.

The building on the southwest corner was built in 1890 by August Rosenberger for his wholesale and retail grocery and feed business. In 1894 a warehouse addition, visible in the earlier photo, was constructed next door. It was razed in the 1940s. The original building is in near-pristine condition outside, thanks to the care of Heldt & Voelker Hardware which has been in it since 1925. Inside, the store is a veritable living museum of retail practice and decor dating back to the 1920s and beyond.

Many of West Franklin Street's older buildings remain, but a number have been lost at an accelerated pace as nearby shopping centers are changing even the ingrained shopping habits of the traditional West Side.

SPECIAL COLLECTIONS, WILLARD LIBRARY OF EVANSVILLE

The Majestic Theater was built on the original site of the Igleheart Brothers mill. The Wabash & Erie Canal entered Evansville along the line of present Canal Street and then turned, in the middle of what is now a Welborn Hospital parking lot, up Fifth Street. In 1856 the three Igleheart Brothers — Asa, William and Levi, Jr. (Asa would later insist on spelling the name Iglehart, without the second "e") — established a large, five-story flour mill on the corner of Fifth Street that is, the canal, and Locust Street. The mill operated there until 1904, long after the canal was a distant memory, when Igleheart Brothers moved to First Avenue, where it and its popular Swans Down Cake Flour

brand would eventually become part of General Foods.

The original mill was demolished and the "New Majestic" Theater was built on the same spot. It was a well-appointed house, although not as pretentious and, with seating for 1,100, not as large as the Grand Theater. It opened on Christmas Day, 1909, and played stock company stage performances and vaudeville. In 1916 movies were added to the vaudeville, and during the 1920s movies were presented almost exclusively.

Next door to the theater was the station of the Evansville, Newburgh and Suburban interurban railway line. Both buildings were lost to urban renewal and replaced by a city-owned parking garage.

UNIVERSITY OF SOUTHERN INDIANA SPECIAL COLLECTIONS / UNIVERSITY ARCHIVES

Vast changes have occurred along Seventh Street — even the name has changed to Martin Luther King Blvd. In the right foreground of the earlier picture is the F.W. Cook Brewery. There is an unwritten law that beer will be brewed wherever there are Germans and a river. Jacob Rice and a partner established their "Old Brewery" in Lamasco in 1837. In 1853, Rice's son and stepson, Louis Rice and Frederick W. Cook, went out on their own and built the "City Brewery" on a cornfield. Four years later the elder Rice bought out the younger. By 1880 the brewery, with its ice houses, malt house, stable, and offices, covered the entire block bounded by Seventh, Sycamore, Eighth, and Main streets. Ultimately the firm became the F.W. Cook Brewing Company, and its most famous label was Cook's "Goldblume." Cook's weathered Prohibition by switching to sparkling soft drinks and (not) near (enough) beer. It lasted more than

C. 1920

a century and went out of business in 1957.

Beyond the brewery is the steeple of Assumption Cathedral. Assumption was Evansville's first Roman Catholic parish, established in 1839 on Second Street. For a number of years it was the only English-speaking Catholic congregation, as the next four parishes — Holy Trinity, St. Mary's, St. Boniface, and St. Anthony's — had German congregations. The new Assumption Church was built beginning in 1872. It became a cathedral when Evansville was established as a separate diocese in 1944.

And beyond Assumption, on the left, is the tower of old Central High School. Nearly all the visible buildings were razed for the construction of the Civic Center and for urban renewal generally.

C. 1995

COLLECTION OF THE EVANSVILLE MUSEUM OF ARTS AND SCIENCE

The U.S. Navy Auxiliary Shipyard at Evansville, operated by a joint venture led by the Missouri Valley Bridge and Iron Company, was just over a year old when the picture on the left was made on Oct. 2, 1943. The first work on the shipyard was a planning session at Evansville's McCurdy Hotel on Feb. 16, 1942, barely two months and a week after Pearl Harbor. In March construction began in an area of scrub trees and shacks on the riverfront between the Mead Johnson Terminal and the SIGECO power plant.

Work on the keel for the first ship, LST157, was begun at International Steel but moved on June 25 to the still unfinished but operational shipyard. "This was not a bad accomplishment," wrote Andrew L. Clark, author of "A Cornfield Shipyard": "six months from conception of the shipyard until it was ready to build ships. Not bad at all, considering the Missouri Valley Bridge and Iron Company and most of the workers had never built a ship before."

At its peak, the shipyard employed as many as 19,500 people. The ships they built, the LST or Landing Ship-Tank, was a 328-foot-long vessel capable of carrying 2100 tons of cargo and discharging it through enormous doors in the bow. Clark writes, "It was a fantastic ship that was

C. 1943

designed to sail the open ocean and still have the ability to beach and retract itself from an enemy shore."

It took 189 days to construct LST157, which was launched on Oct. 31, 1942. Speed and efficiency increased until the Evansville workers were capable of turning out 20 ships in 61 days. The Evansville shipyard built a total of 167 LSTs, more than at similar yards in Pittsburgh, in Jeffersonville, Ind., and in Seneca, Ill. The Evansville workers proudly claimed the title "World's Champion LST Builders."

The last Evansville-built LST, LST1110, was commissioned on Feb. 28, 1945, although the shipyard continued making other kinds of vessels. It closed almost as soon as Japan surrendered, and fire destroyed most of the buildings on Jan. 26, 1946. The site is now a Mead Johnson parking lot, still called the "shipyard" lot. A few traces of the shipyard can still be seen, especially at low water. There is a commemorative stone marker at the Ohio Street entrance.

The Evansville Museum exhibits a large model of an LST, has more than 10,000 official Navy photographs of shipyard operations in its archives and also owns the flag that LST157, Evansville's first-launched LST, flew during the D-Day invasion at Normandy on June 6, 1944.

UNIVERSITY OF SOUTHERN INDIANA SPECIAL COLLECTIONS / UNIVERSITY ARCHIVES

The Soldiers and Sailors Memorial Coliseum at Fourth and Court streets was one of Mayor Benjamin Bosse's many "brick and mortar" projects. It was built in 1916-17 as a tribute to the Vanderburgh County men who had fought in the Civil War and the Spanish American War. It was dedicated on April 18, 1917, two days after the United States declared war on Germany in World War I.

Designed by Clifford Shopbell, Bosse's favorite architect, the Coliseum was an all-purpose facility. It hosted concerts, including those of the Evansville Philharmonic Orchestra; trade shows, including an annual automobile show; conventions of all sorts of groups; professional and amateur plays; lectures; political rallies; corporate meetings and parties and even the Shrine Circus. In other words, it was the venue for the same types of events that are now scattered among Roberts Stadium, Mesker Amphitheater, Vanderburgh Auditorium and Green Convention Center. The Coliseum even attempted movies after a local theater owner sold the county his used projection equipment. Unfortunately it was a "silent" projector, being sold because the theater was converting to "talkies."

The two statuary groups on either side of the columned entrance were done by Evansville sculptor George Honig. On the left, "The Spirit of 1861," the Union soldiers defend Liberty and the flag. On the right, "The Spirit of 1916," the

two old veterans sit on a park bench retelling war stories as Liberty crowns them with heroes' laurel.

The Coliseum is now managed and under restoration by the Council of Veterans Organizations. It still hosts various events but is best known today for Wednesday night wrestling.

Bosse was elected mayor three times and served from 1914 until he died in office on April 4, 1922. Appropriately, he lay in state at the Coliseum, and the picture on the left shows the crowd gathered to witness the transfer of his body to Trinity Lutheran Church for the funeral. Lowe's Funeral Home provided the city's first motorized hearse for the occasion.

At left in both pictures is the old Liederkranz Maennerchor building constructed in 1911. Liederkranz was one of three Evansville German singing societies. The others were the Germania and the Concordia, of which only Germania, with its Octoberfest-in-August Volksfest, remains. During World War I, German clubs like the Liederkranz had to "limit their activities." The hall was sold to the Knights of Columbus. Later it was for a time the Republican Party headquarters.

St. John's United Church of Christ was destroyed by fire between the two photos. The older and newer editions of its steeple are visible over the left corner of the Coliseum.

SPECIAL COLLECTIONS, WILLARD LIBRARY OF EVANSVILLE

In 1890 readers learned, "There is no manufacturing establishment in the city of Evansville which The Courier would rather mention in this paper than the Blount Plow works, inasmuch as it is one of our most prominent manufactories. The stranger walking on outer Main Street (at Illinois Street) would not fail to remark upon the mammoth building, occupied by this concern. It is a splendid brick edifice of 125 by 300 feet in dimensions, the ground covering an entire square."

Founded in 1867 by Henry F. Blount, the company made several kinds of farm implements but was best known for "Blount's True Blue," a revolutionary plow with a steel point that could be removed for sharpening. The company produced 12,000 such plows a year. Theodore Dreiser, who lived just a few blocks away, wrote of Blount's Plow Works in the 1880s, "with giant hammers

C. 1900

beating steel bars into ploughshares and belching flame and smoke, often by night as well as by day."

In 1876 Blount became the first president of the Willard Library Board of Trustees, and a portrait of him hangs in the library's board room. By 1886, he was a 57-year-old millionaire. He retired from active management of his company, moved to Georgetown, D.C., and in 1890 purchased an estate then known merely as "The Oaks" but more famous in later years as "Dumbarton Oaks."

Blount Plow eventually became Burch Plow when it was owned and operated by A.V. Burch and his sons. It moved to Evansville's far north, off U.S. 41, in the late 1960s, was ultimately purchased by Chromalloy and by the mid-1980s had faded from the scene entirely. The old factory at Main and Illinois streets was razed and replaced by a Great Scot and later a Buehler's Buy-Low supermarket.

HIGHWAY 66 LAYING THE CONCRETE SLAB THROUGH NEWBURG IND. MAY

COLLECTIONS OF THE OHIO TOWNSHIP PUBLIC LIBRARY, NEWBURGH

Workers were building Indiana 66 (later Indiana 662) through Newburgh on May 5, 1930. It is said that one of the Newburgh druggists used his influence to have the highway routed through the village's downtown and, not necessarily coincidentally, through his next-door competitor's store on the northeast corner of State and Jennings streets.

The S-curve that took the highway from Jennings to the riverside did carefully avoid the Methodist Church, however. The congregation has since moved a couple of miles north on State Street, and the former church is now the Riverwalk Condominium apartments.

C. 1995

COLLECTIONS OF THE OHIO TOWNSHIP PUBLIC LIBRARY, NEWBURGH

The Citizens Bank Building was erected on the southeast corner of State and Jennings streets in Newburgh in 1902. It had become the Farmers Bank of Newburgh by 1918, when the building was expanded to twice its size and extensively remodeled.

Three years later the bank was found to be insolvent, and its assets "wasted and improperly converted." Officials absconded and investors committed suicide. In short it was a big mess and scandal for such a small town.

The bank's remaining property was conveyed to the State Bank of Newburgh in November 1921. That organization was absorbed into Warrick

C. 1910

National Bank (since absorbed in turn by Old National Bank), which vacated the building and moved five blocks up State Street in 1967.

For a time the old bank building housed Newburgh Galleries, an interior decorating studio. Most recently it has been the location of the Sprinklesburgh Village gift shops, so called after the original name of Newburgh. Business was suspended in November 1993, due to complications from damage during the disastrous fire at The Landing Restaurant at the opposite end of the block.

C. 1935

PHOTOGRAPH COURTESY JAMES RODE

The names of several Evansville streets — Allen Lane, for example, or Martin's Lane — suggest their origin as farm lanes. The main building of the 40-acre Arden Dairy farm, operated by Henry and Anna Boeke, stood at the present intersection of Morgan Avenue and, appropriately, Boeke Road.

The area developed quickly as the city spread east after World War II. The Arden site is now dominated by a fast-food restaurant, a gasoline/convenience store and an apartment complex. The Boeke's farmhouse, built in 1906, has been moved to a residential area several blocks away.

Newcomers to Evansville are easy to spot until they learn that "Boeke" is pronounced "Bakey" rather than "Boak."

PHOTOGRAPH COURTESY HELEN ELI

In the 1950s, when Kentucky Avenue was still U.S. 41, Evansville's hot summers were more bearable when you could pile the children into the family Hudson (or is it a Nash?) and enjoy a frosty root beer at the Dog 'n Suds.

In the evenings teen-agers with cars, or with friends with cars, could cruise the series of drive-in restaurants along Kentucky Avenue, from Austin's in the north between Sycamore and Walnut streets, past the Humpty-Dumpty south of Riverside Drive, to the Farmer's Daughter and, across the street, the Dog 'n Suds in the 2200 block.

At the south end of the street was another kind of drive-in, the Family Drive In Theatre.

The smiling uniformed "carhop" pictured ready to bring out the root beer, hot dogs and floats is Marie Steinsultz, now Marie Hall, who was a sweet 16 when this picture was taken in 1956. Nowadays cars drive into (and out of) a used car lot at that location.

C. 1956

C. 1995

From 1914 to 1916 Evansville's three major banks all built impressive new buildings on Main Street. National City Bank (then City National) opened the building it still occupies at Third and Main streets on Jan. 1, 1914. Old National Bank moved into its new six-story, later nine-story, building at Fifth and Main streets, across the street from the bank's present location, on July 29, 1916.

Between the two, chronologically and geographically, was Citizens National Bank's new 10-story headquarters, opened at Fourth and Main streets, Evansville's busiest commercial corner and most expensive

COLLECTION OF THE EVANSVILLE MUSEUM OF ARTS AND SCIENCE

C. 1920s

real estate, on Feb. 22, 1916.

Evansville's first tall steel-frame structure, it could also claim to be the city's first skyscraper, although that term is used loosely in Evansville.

The bank has since moved twice, to a new building at 19 NW Fourth St. in 1959 and then in the 1980s to its present building at Third and Sycamore streets. In the meantime, under successive management, the old building has been known as the Southern Securities Building, the Commerce Building and now the Hilliard-Lyons Building. The exterior has changed little in nearly eight decades.

SPECIAL COLLECTIONS, WILLARD LIBRARY OF EVANSVILLE

At Main and Michigan streets once stood an unusual offshoot of Evansville's hardwood lumber industry. In 1890 The Evansville Courier wrote, "There is probably no firm in this city that is as widely known in the Southern and Western States as the Evansville Coffin Co. It was incorporated in 1881 with a capital of $25,000 and has annually increased its trade until today they have few peers among their competitors in the United States.

"The manufacture of coffins has undergone a

C. 1890

great change during the last half century, and in this revolution fashion has been the great motive power. Now as much taste and elegance of finish are required in the manufacture of a burial casket as in the construction of a piece of household furniture, and the very finest of wood is used. — Sixty skilled workmen are employed in the factory, and even then they can hardly keep up with their orders."

The Evansville Coffin Co. went out of business in 1928. A recently refurbished branch of National City Bank is now on the same site.

SPECIAL COLLECTIONS, WILLARD LIBRARY OF EVANSVILLE

One of the little quirks designed to confuse new Evansville residents is the fact that Bosse Field is not at Bosse High School; Enlow Field is. The ballpark actually predated the school, the latter being named after Mayor Benjamin Bosse following his death, the former being named for him while he was still very much alive.

The baseball field was a school board project, built on the southeast corner of Garvin Park, which the Bosse administration was developing out of Thomas Garvin's former picnic grove. Historian James Morlock wrote that the stadium "was named Bosse Field in honor of the mayor who had given great encouragement and support to the development of an athletic program." It is well to remember also that in those days the school board members were appointed by the mayor, so as far as the board was concerned, Bosse was the Boss.

Bosse Field was dedicated on June 17, 1915, with an overflow crowd of 8,082 having to resort to standing room in the outfield. The next day The Courier reported that "Evansville quit work yesterday at noon and swung into one of the gayest holidays in its memory to fittingly commemorate the official dedication of Bosse Field, the finest

athletic field in Indiana — The crowd which filled the great oval was unparalleled in the history of Evansville athletic events — when the speeches and ceremonies were over, the crowd roared 'Play ball' — Punch Knoll led his team, resplendent in black and white striped uniforms onto the diamond — Mayor Bosse pitched the first ball — Evansville won the game from Erie in a nip and tuck pitcher's duel, score 4-0."

That opening game was not a school contest but a professional game among teams of the "Three-I League." A succession of "farm" teams have played at Bosse Field, including most recently the Evansville Braves, the Triplets, and, after several years' hiatus, now the Otters.

The fact that few obvious changes have been made in Bosse Field over the years made it a natural location for the filming of the recent Hollywood film, "A League of Their Own." Between these 1921 and 1995 photos, supporting posts were moved, the stone wall separating the stands from the field was replaced by a brick wall, new dugouts were built and lights were added to allow night games.

There is today an active Friends of Bosse Field organization dedicated to preserving the stadium and its traditions.

C. 1995

PHOTOGRAPHY COURTESY BARBARA LEACH

Motor traffic between Evansville and Henderson, Ky., used to require passage on a small ferry at the end of Old Henderson Road in Union Township. That changed with the U.S. 41 bridge, which was under construction in 1931 when Ethel Butsch had her photograph taken on the north shore.

Kentucky announced plans for a bridge in 1928, and despite the fact that, because of an anomaly of river geography, the entire bridge is within the boundaries of the Commonwealth, the State of Indiana offered to pay half of its construction costs. As it turned out, after much negotiation and a "friendly" suit between the two states, the bridge ended up being paid for half by the federal government and half by motorists' tolls.

C. 1932

Construction began in the spring of 1931. The center span of the finished bridge was 600 feet long, and the length of the steel structure is more than a mile. The governors of Indiana and Kentucky dedicated the bridge on July 4, 1932. Tolls ended on March 20, 1941, after motorists had handed over their half of the $2.5 million cost.

After three decades of one-bridge, two-way traffic, by the 1960s the number of cars and trucks prompted plans for a parallel bridge downstream from the original. Although the official name of the bridge is the "Tri-State Vietnam Gold Star Memorial Bridge," this vital north-south link is universally known colloquially as the "Twin Bridges."

SPECIAL COLLECTIONS, WILLARD LIBRARY OF EVANSVILLE

Grandly named The Temple of Fine Arts, the Evansville Museum functioned in the old Joseph Setchell residence on Second Street between Vine and Court streets from 1928 until it moved into its present building on the riverbank in 1959.

Actually, the move to Sunset Park was a kind of homecoming for the museum, which had begun on the same site, in the old Robert Barnes mansion, in 1904. The city peremptorily declared the building unsafe in 1910 and demolished it. The museum's collections were dispersed in various places; some of them found temporary exhibit space on the then-unused top floor of Willard Library.

In 1927-28, the YWCA, which had been in the Setchell house, built a new building next door, facing Vine Street. This left the Setchell house

available for the Museum, which moved in in April 1928. The cultural diaspora was over and the scattered collections were called home. Legend has it that some objets d'art never made it back, the families who had given them shelter in 1910 having come to believe in the meantime that they had always owned them.

On the distant skyline, left of center, can be seen the statue of the Roman god Vulcan atop the Vulcan Plow Company at First and Ingle streets. After the building was razed the statue spent time in the backyard of a First Street home before being installed in the Old Courthouse basement. From roof to ground level to basement — how the mighty are fallen!

The old YWCA/museum site is now a parking lot, where Evansville newspaper employees parked when their offices were across the street.

DEACONESS HOSPITAL ARCHIVE

A movement to recruit young women as nurses, or "deaconesses," began in Germany in 1836 and traveled to America in the wake of German immigration. In May 1893, the Protestant Deaconess Association purchased a frame home at Mary and Iowa streets from Major Byron Parsons and established a 19-bed hospital. The home had already achieved some distinction when Clara Barton, founder of the American Red Cross, stayed with the Parsonses and used their house as the headquarters for the Red Cross' first big domestic relief effort during the devastating 1884 Ohio River flood.

In 1897 the Parsons house was moved to the back of its lot and a new Deaconess Hospital was con-

C. 1948

structed on the corner. It was still extant in 1948, though without the exquisite little cupola that originally capped it. Both the Parsons house and the 1897 hospital were subsumed by further hospital expansion. A physicians' office complex was under construction on the old hospital site in 1995.

Parenthetically it might be noted that at exactly the same time the Protestant deaconesses were establishing their hospital on Mary Street, the Catholic Daughters of Charity were moving their 20-year-old hospital from Ohio Street to First Avenue and Columbia Street. The two sectarian hospitals operated within a couple of blocks of each other until 1956, when St. Mary's moved to the far East Side.

C. 1995

UNIVERSITY OF SOUTHERN INDIANA SPECIAL COLLECTIONS / UNIVERSITY ARCHIVES

Cow pasture surrounded the Evansville Cotton Mill in the late 1800s. The factory, formerly located Downtown, moved to a giant new factory on St. Joseph Avenue near the river in 1875. It was reported that it was "equipped as well as any in the country, all being new and of the most approved and improved style known. — The motive power is supplied by a Corliss engine of 350 horse-power, and eight tubular boilers. 14,000 spindles, 400 looms, 110 cards are kept in operation, besides a full complement of drawing frames, lappens and coarse and fine speeders, requiring the labors of 300 hands."

To house some of those hands, in 1876 Charles Viele and other investors built the cotton mill tenements next door, which are the double row of

three-story buildings at the right edge of the picture.

The cotton mill ceased operations after the turn of the century. E. Mead Johnson was looking for a replacement for his burned-out New Jersey infant-food factory when, legend has it, he spotted the abandoned cotton mill through a train window. Mead Johnson Company started operations there March 1, 1916.

The mill and its tenements have long since disappeared as Mead Johnson has demolished, built, and expanded. The cow pastures have disappeared, too, as Mead Johnson and the 1918 Reitz High School spurred residential construction up and down Reitz Hill.

PHOTOGRAPH COURTESY CHESTER T. BEHRMAN

A general store owned and operated by Michael Bauer, one of the many German immigrants who flooded into the area in the 1840s, stood for decades at the corner of Darmstadt Road and Boonville-New Harmony Road. Bauer's store later became Scherzinger's Grocery, and much of the exterior of the building remained, including the porch and wooden columns. It served the Darmstadt area until early in 1963 when it was destroyed by fire. Today, the Village Square Shopping Center occupies the same corner.

The Bauer name is still associated with Darmstadt in the form of the Bauer's Grove Bauerhaus catering and meeting center, "115 years of service."

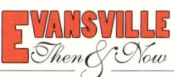

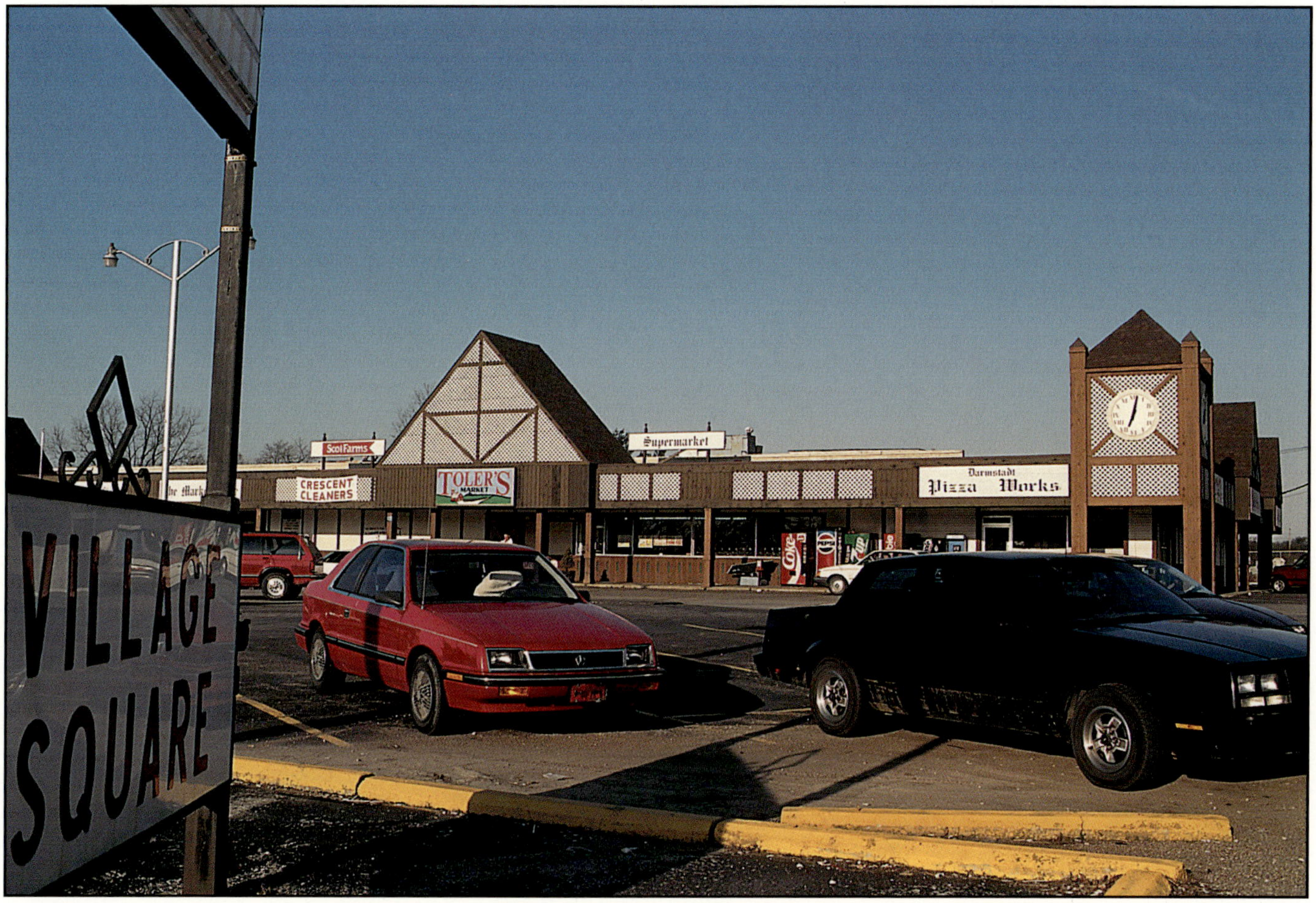
VILLAGE SQUARE
CRESCENT CLEANERS
TOLER'S
Supermarket
Darmstadt Pizza Works

C. 1995

COLLECTION OF THE EVANSVILLE MUSEUM OF ARTS AND SCIENCE

The well-known J.F. Bomm Drug Company was about to close in 1923 after years of doing business at Fifth and Main streets. Its neighbors toward the river were The Hub ("exclusive hats and furnishings for men and boys"), S.S. Kresge's "5¢ to 25¢ Store" and the Boston Store, dry goods, Fowler, Dick, and Walker, proprietors.

In 1995, Sun Optical Company occupies the Bomm location and, under all the remodeling, the

Bomm building. The next two original buildings are also present, although likewise barely recognizable. The Boston Store building was the location in more recent memory of the Darling Shop and Neisner Brothers' "5¢ to $1" store. Although that structure fell to urban renewal and is now a parking lot, when longtime Evansville residents pass that site they can still almost smell the caramel corn odor which Neisner's used to entice customers into the store.

SPECIAL COLLECTIONS, WILLARD LIBRARY OF EVANSVILLE

SPECIAL COLLECTIONS, WILLARD LIBRARY OF EVANSVILLE

— C. 1925 & 1910 —

SPECIAL COLLECTIONS, WILLARD LIBRARY OF EVANSVILLE

Two splendid hotels have graced the corner of First and Locust streets in the past 120 years. Opened with a Mardi Gras Ball on Feb. 19, 1874, the steam-heated, elevator-equipped St. George Hotel had a bathroom on each of its five guest floors. Although the elevator reached the upper floors "in a twinkling," room rates decreased from $2.50 to $2 per day as one went upward.

Meals were 75 cents, and one enraptured reporter felt the cuisine "is its chief glory. Everything palatable that flies, walks, swims or crawls, in air, water or earth is furnished. Everything that grows deep down in the soil, or is suspended from bough or vine is supplied in abundance."

By the early 1900s, style, convenience, and technology had all left the St. George behind. In January 1915, people gathered to say a fond farewell. Mayor Benjamin Bosse spoke, and socialite soprano Amy Morgan Viele sang "The Last Rose of Summer." The St. George was razed and a new, U-shaped, eight-story hotel took its place. Named for Col. William H. McCurdy, local industrialist and investor in the enterprise, the new hotel was operated by Fred and F. Harold Van Orman, father and son. The hotelier's style being not much different from that of the politician, the younger Van Orman was elected Indiana's lieutenant governor and served from 1925 to 1929.

During the 1970s the hotel was converted to a residential and nursing facility for the aged.

The "home" of the Benevolent and Protective Order of Elks across the street was 10 years older than the McCurdy. It had become the Upstage Dinner Theater by the time it was destroyed in a fire-and-ice conflagration in sub-zero weather in 1977.

C. 1995

SPECIAL COLLECTIONS, WILLARD LIBRARY OF EVANSVILLE

One of the major achievements of the Mayor Benjamin Bosse era was convincing Moores Hill College to move to Evansville from southeastern Indiana after its principal building was destroyed by fire. Businessman George S. Clifford raised enough civic and monetary support to see the project through despite having to compete with World War I Liberty Bond drives. Methodist-run Evansville College started classes in September 1919, in Adath Israel Synagogue's school building on Vine Street.

An ambitious master-plan for a collegiate-gothic

East Side campus was drawn up. Part of that plan was the Administration Building and its oval approach drive off Lincoln Avenue. Under construction at the time of the photograph, the Indiana limestone building was completed by May 1922. Later named for longtime administrator and institutional historian Ralph Olmstead, the building remains virtually unchanged on its exterior except for the addition of an ungainly antenna tower.

Evansville College became the University of Evansville in 1967.

SPECIAL COLLECTIONS, WILLARD LIBRARY OF EVANSVILLE

Evansville mercantilist Cadwalader M. Griffith built this house at 514 SE First St. around the time he was elected to the first City Council after Evansville received its city charter in 1847. Griffith also served as county probate judge in 1850-51.

At about the same time that Griffith was building, druggist Crawford Bell erected a very similar home at 506 SE First St.. For a decade or more these two houses remained alone on that block on

what was then Evansville's far Southeast Side.

Over the years the Griffith house has acquired close neighbors and an enclosed front porch. The earlier photo, taken when the house was a mere half-century or so old, shows it with a typical Victorian fence. Not only did such good fences make good neighbors but they also kept the horses out of the front yards. It is said most of the city's iron fences were contributed to the scrap metal drives of World War I and World War II.

![Brewery photo]

SPECIAL COLLECTIONS, WILLARD LIBRARY OF EVANSVILLE

The brewery at Fulton Avenue and Pennsylvania Street/Lloyd Expressway is easily recognized in both photographs. The building has acquired an addition or two, chimneys having been lowered, and windows having been bricked up. On the other hand, bricks (and trolley tracks) have disappeared from the street. Despite the appearance of stoplights and the intersection's reputation as a bottleneck, traffic moves faster in 1995.

The Fulton Avenue Brewery was formed in 1877 by Wilhelm Ullmer of Russia and Ferdinand Hoedt of the German state of Baden. By 1880 it was reported, "Their capital was small, but most judiciously placed, and within a space of less than thirty months have they been enabled to so increase it as to add one of the handsomest and most complete breweries to the beauty and wealth of our lovely city. — The brewery will have a cellar capacity of 3,000 barrels constantly on hand, and a selling capacity of 18,000 barrels per annum. — The new brewery — will contain all the latest improvements, which have so materially added to give beer its present incomparable qualities."

The brewery's special "export" beer was particu-

C. 1910

larly fine: "So universal are the good qualities of this famous beer, especially for purity and such health-giving and preserving qualities as it possesses, that there is scarcely a family, no matter how temperate, that has not at some time experienced its pleasant and beneficial effects."

Somewhat later the Evansville Brewing Association merged into the Fulton Avenue Brewery, bringing its already established Sterling brand with it. Sterling was also supposed to have healthful effects, particularly on the lower digestive tract — "if nature won't, Sterling will," 'twas said — but the company did not care to emphasize that characteristic in its advertising.

Indeed, it accused its rivals at Cook's Brewery of surreptitiously spreading an untruth.

In the 1980s the brewery was "sold out of town" to the G. Heileman Brewery of Lacrosse, Wis., which subsequently declared it too old and inefficient and shut it down. After the brewery sat idle for a time, local investors formed a new Evansville Brewing Company and once again beer was — and is — made on the old corner, not just under the Sterling label but also under the labels of several old German/Rivertown beers, including Weidemann's of Cincinnati, Falls City of Louisville, Ky., and even Sterling's former local rival, Cook's "Goldblume."

COLLECTION OF THE EVANSVILLE MUSEUM OF ARTS AND SCIENCE

At a crest of 48.40 feet, the flood of March-April 1913 was Evansville's biggest flood before 1937. The stone item surrounded by water at center left is a monument to Capt. Henry T. Dexter, who arrived at the Evansville riverfront with his boat, the Charley Bowen, on Nov. 11, 1858. Steamboats regularly arrived at Evansville, promising to make the city their "home port," only to up anchor and chug off into the sunset if business did not meet expectations. Dexter had no such intentions. Even before leaving his place on the upper deck, he shouted to the assembled citizenry, "We have come to stay."

During the next 14 years Dexter captained and/or owned, alone or in partnership, a number of Evansville boats — the Charmer, Superior, Courier, Armada, and Arkansas Belle. His crowning achievement was to be the ill-fated City of Evansville, which included among its decorations paintings of "Capt. Dexter's advent in these waters with the Charley Bowen" and "Dexter pointing out to his sweetheart the beauties of the city of Evansville." The new steamer arrived in Evansville on March 7, 1870, only to perish eight months later in a spectacular fire that also consumed two other steamers and the Evansville wharfboat.

During the Civil War, Dexter armed the Charley Bowen with a four-pounder cannon, and on one occasion he used it to face down a Confederate-sympathizing crowd at Paducah, Ky., which demanded he lower the United States flag. Standing next to the cannon, Dexter dared the mob to "lower it, if you dare."

After the war Dexter used the little cannon as a hitching post in front of his Locust Street home. After his death in 1872, the cannon was incorporated into the Dexter monument, which was placed square in the intersection of Main and Water streets. Over the years it became an infor-

mal flood gauge. Whenever water crept up the monument's base, its crest was duly marked and dated. This undoubtedly settled many a saloon dispute over whether this year's "high water" was higher than last year's. The monument is now on the Evansville Museum grounds.

None of the buildings visible in the 1913 picture are present in the 1995 view. The difference between old "walking cities" and contemporary "driving cities" is evident.

C. 1995

SPECIAL COLLECTIONS, WILLARD LIBRARY OF EVANSVILLE

On March 24, 1953, the one-millionth Plymouth built in Indiana rolled through the assembly line at Evansville's Chrysler plant on Stringtown Road. The Plymouth model was only a year old when Chrysler arrived in Evansville to assemble Plymouths at the old Graham Truck factory in 1935. Its body works, Briggs Indiana Corporation, took over the former Graham Automobile factory on East Columbia Street, and cars-in-the-making traveled a private road between the two factories.

Chrysler and Briggs soon employed 5,000 people, an economic boon in Depression times. There was a hiatus during World War II when Chrysler became an ordnance plant making "billions of bullets." Consumer demand for cars unavailable during the war encouraged the Evansville plants to turn out as many as 400 cars a day in the post-war years. Many of the cars were shipped by barge to the Gulf states and the southwest.

Occasionally a barge would capsize, and people in the downriver towns have stories of relatives who got a new Plymouth cheap by right of salvage.

Chrysler was Evansville's biggest employer when it began phasing out local operations in 1959 in favor of a new factory in Fenton, Mo. One of the executives who had to participate in that decision was 1935 Bosse High School graduate Lynn Townsend, who in 1961 would move up to president of Chrysler at age 42.

The loss of Chrysler and Briggs was part of a series of plant closings and mergers that had some people in the late 1950s fearing that Evansville was facing economic doomsday. Fortunately, other companies arrived to take up the slack.

This part of the old Chrysler plant, since expanded, is occupied by Indian Industries, Inc., and houses a machine to make components for ping-pong tables.

SPECIAL COLLECTIONS, WILLARD LIBRARY OF EVANSVILLE

Thanks to nearly 30 years of preservation on a shoestring by the Old Courthouse Preservation Society, the Old Vanderburgh County Courthouse appears largely unchanged since its completion in 1890. Located on the site of a formerly warehouse-ringed basin of the Wabash & Erie Canal, it took the place of the previous courthouse at Third and Main streets.

It was designed by Louisville architect Henry Wolters, and in its Beaux Arts grandeur it was meant to portray in Indiana limestone the prosperity and power of Victorian Evansville. In a commemorative book written in 1972, the preservation group wrote that most people had done government business there without stopping "to look up to see what irreplaceable beauty is actually there. Like Notre Dame in Paris, Westminster Abbey in London, and dozens of other famous landmarks in Europe, our courthouse is the kind of building so encrusted with sculpture and stone carvings that one cannot take it all in at once. — There are not only 14 main statues of human figures, there are the national emblems, the great seal of the State of Indiana, ornamental friezes, fat little cherubs —, and countless garlands and wreaths (all different) of flowers, leaves, nuts,

fruits, and vegetables that are indigenous to this area."

The 14 statues in four groupings were the work of a Chicago German-American sculptor named Franz Engelsmann. They are allegories of the "Superman" values — truth, justice, and the American way.

The Old Courthouse was left behind when the Civic Center opened in 1969. To pay expenses, the Preservation Society (formerly the Conrad Baker Foundation) has rented space in the building for all kinds of enterprises in the years since, including at times antique stores, restaurants, dance troupes and theater companies. For the most part it has served as an office building, which is what a courthouse actually is. In the most recent months, ironically, the Civic Center has become overcrowded and a few county functions are making their way back to the Old Courthouse.

On the right edge of both pictures is the 1914 YMCA building, now vacant.

C. 1995

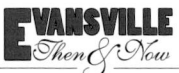

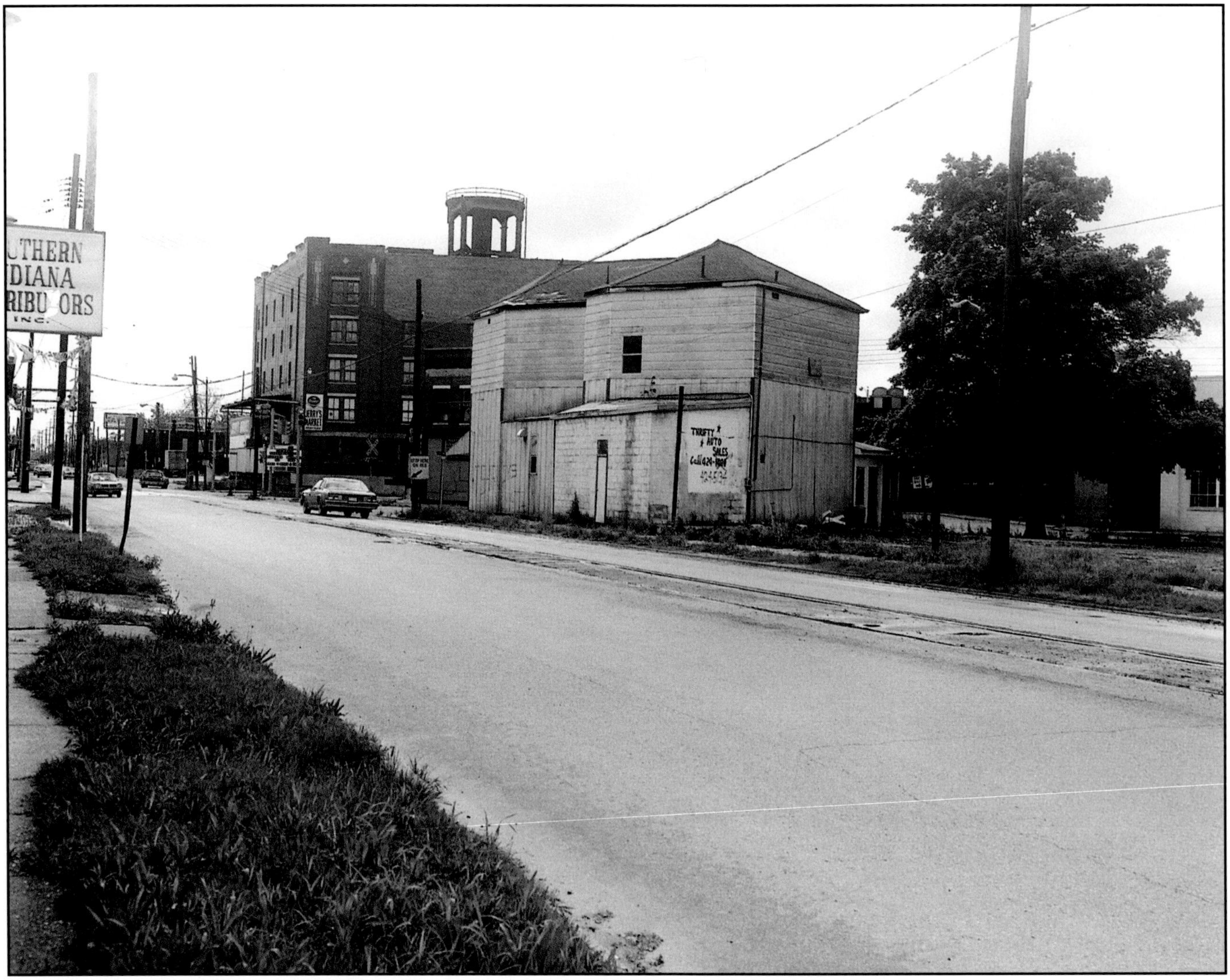

UNIVERSITY OF SOUTHERN INDIANA SPECIAL COLLECTIONS / UNIVERSITY ARCHIVES

This is Division Street, looking west toward Main Street. The buildings on the south side of the street, including T and Shirley's Bar in the foreground and a Jerry's Market in the large, brick former Hulman Warehouse building behind, were demolished when the Lloyd Expressway was built in the 1980s. The railroad tracks were also finally taken up.

Division/Pennsylvania Street was always a main thoroughfare because, although it changed names

C. 1979

in the middle of its run, it was the only street in town that went all the way from the East Side to the West Side. Finding a train coming at one down the middle of the street was a very disconcerting experience for a century's worth of Evansville teamsters and motorists. The mayor rode a so-called "last train down Division Street" in 1973, but the L&N would occasionally send trains down the old route almost to the day the builders of the Lloyd cut the tracks. Cars move somewhat faster now, even off the Expressway.

COLLECTION OF THE EVANSVILLE MUSEUM OF ARTS AND SCIENCE

Evansville was a coal-burning and sometimes smoky river city in the pre-Environmental Protection Agency era when this photograph was made from the roof of the Furniture (Court) Building around 1914. At the center of the photograph, at Fourth and Sycamore streets, stands the building the YMCA vacated that year.

This view is now dominated by the roof of the old Sears Building (now occupied by subsidiary operations of Old National Bank) and the Hulman building, which stands where the Y once stood. Two landmarks remain: the twin spires of Trinity United Methodist Church in the upper left, and just to the right of those, the steeple of First Presbyterian Church in the vague, smoggy distance.

C. 1914

C. 1995

UNIVERSITY OF SOUTHERN INDIANA SPECIAL COLLECTIONS / UNIVERSITY ARCHIVES

If some Evansville Rip Van Winkle were to awaken, he would still recognize the scene on Riverside Drive between Chestnut and Cherry streets. As a 1919 program book for a convention of traveling salesmen — Evansville's economic lifelines to the outside world — noted, "stately mansions — are not unusual in this city of refinement and wealth." The city's "leafy avenues, flanked by dignified homes, reflects (sic) the gentility of its people."

The house at Riverside Drive and Cherry Street was built by dry goods merchant Charles Viele in 1856 and extensively remodeled in the latest French Second Empire style in 1873, after the Viele family took the Grand Tour of Europe. Paintings by starving European artists filled the house and statues by starving European sculptors filled the yard.

After the turn of the century, coalman Jabez

C. 1925

Wooley built his house in what had been the Viele's side yard, where their conservatory had once stood. The mid-19th century Richard Raleigh house next door, with its wonderful three-story French-Quarter-style iron porch, has become a "bed and breakfast" inn.

John G. Venneman built his house on the far corner, at Riverside Drive and Chestnut Street in 1870. After the turn of the century a tower, reminiscent of Italian church campaniles, was added to accommodate a residential elevator.

On the river side of Riverside Drive can be seen an edge of the Robert Barnes mansion, one of Evansville's earliest stately homes. The Evansville Museum occupied it from 1904 to 1910, when the city declared the building structurally unsound and demolished it. The museum returned to the site in 1959.

SPECIAL COLLECTIONS, WILLARD LIBRARY OF EVANSVILLE

Originally constructed as a theater-hotel combination, the Victory Theater and Sonntag Hotel structure still stands on the corner of Sixth and Main streets. The Victory opened on July 16, 1921, and survived to become the last Downtown movie house remaining after urban renewal. Kenneth P. McCutchan has written in his "At the Bend in the River" that at the Victory "Evansville residents enjoyed first-run pictures, classy vaudeville acts accompanied by a 15-piece orchestra, and entre-act music played on the great pipe organ. The house seated 2,600 and became the most popular entertainment house in the city — also one of the first public buildings

C. 1941

to install central air conditioning. It was a real treat to walk by the Victory Theater on a hot summer afternoon and catch a breath of the damp, water-cooled air that came out when the foyer doors were open."

The Victory kept going until 1979, when films ended and the facility embarked on a new career as first a disco and then a sometimes "night club" for teen-agers. It is now the subject of a fund drive to restore the theater as a concert/performance hall.

The Sonntag, rechristened the Civic Plaza, operated as an ever more seedy residential hotel until 1985, when its boiler gave out. At present it is proposed that it be converted into an educational facility.

SPECIAL COLLECTIONS, WILLARD LIBRARY OF EVANSVILLE

Dade Park has long since become Ellis Park. The grandstand still stands, even more grandly.

When built in 1928, the thoroughbred racing track was the only totally legal enterprise among the somewhat naughty entertainments handy to Evansville on the "no-man's land" of Kentucky property on the north side of the river. There were also nightclubs of various repute, the most

famous among them the Trocadero, across the road from the track. Especially after the discovery of oil in 1938 brought high-rolling petroleum barons to town, they could literally roll high in the gambling room upstairs at the "Troc," while downstairs they could dance to the best big band music. The Trocadero had a more sedate retirement career as an antique mall until it burned to the ground a few years ago.

SPECIAL COLLECTIONS, WILLARD LIBRARY OF EVANSVILLE

In a model of "swift and certain" justice, John Harvey was sentenced on June 7, 1823, for the murder of a man named Casey and was hanged on June 27. The gallows were erected on the southwest corner of Third and Main streets, across from the first brick courthouse (which was on the site of the present National City Bank). Harvey was summarily buried on the site.

Thirty years later, laborers digging the foundations for the Washington House Hotel discovered Harvey's bones. A local physician claimed them, wired them together, and hung Harvey in his office. As the practice was passed to each succeeding generation of doctor, so was Harvey's skeleton. The remains of Evansville's first convicted murderer can now be seen as part of the pioneer doctor's office in the Old Rivertown exhibit at the Evansville Museum.

The Washington House opened in 1855 and was at the time one of the finest hotels in the young river city. An early advertisement promised, "A watch is kept for steam boats at all hours, day and night." That meant guests would have enough

C. 1916

warning to get packed and to the landing before the boat left again. In addition, "passengers arriving by the night train can procure supper at this house."

The building was put to numerous other uses through the years. It acquired its French Second Empire mansard roof during an 1878 remodeling when the nearly 30-year-old Evansville Commercial College, a private school of business practice, moved in. It was still there in 1890, offering "practical education of both sexes for the active duties of life," particularly "every variety and style of bookkeeping" as well as "penmanship, short-hand writing, commercial calculations, business correspondence, mercantile law, etc."

In more recent memory real mercantile pursuits held sway in the building, including a Thom McAn shoe store. The layer of stuccolike material was applied in 1963, when the Farmer's Daughter Restaurant moved in. In 1995, radio station WVHI called the building home, but the restaurant was no more.

SPECIAL COLLECTIONS, WILLARD LIBRARY OF EVANSVILLE

The houses, shacks, and rooftops of a close-packed city cluttered this view of Downtown looking east from the roof of the Furniture Exchange Building (now the Court Building) earlier this century. The F.W. Cook Brewing Company on Seventh Street is seen in the distance, at center left. Little other than the ledge of the Court Building roof remains recognizable. Downtown has changed from an area scaled to people to one more friendly to automobiles.

C. 1914

C. 1995

PHOTOGRAPHY COURTESY DON BAUMGART

In the winter of 1941 a snow-covered farmhouse stood at what is now the intersection of Green River Road and Virginia Street. The home belonged to Victor J. Baumgart, who along with his brother, grew wheat, corn, barley and oats on 90 acres of farmland east of Green River Road. The farm has more recently sprouted buildings in the commercial expansion of the area. A large restaurant now stands where the small house was once located.

SPECIAL COLLECTIONS, WILLARD LIBRARY OF EVANSVILLE

A 1956 aerial view of Evansville's riverfront shows a Downtown packed with buildings. Urban renewal and the Southlane Drive project would soon take many of them. A few notable exceptions are the McCurdy Hotel/Residential Center, at right, the Old Post Office at left-center, and the old Citizens Bank/Hilliard-Lyons Building in the middle of the muddle.

The contemporary photograph illustrates the city with the riverfront renewal area finally being filled in to some extent by new structures — a condominium, office buildings, television station,

restaurant/bar disguised as a steamboat — built in the 1980s and 1990s. The 1980s Esplanade project refurbished the old Dress Plaza as an area more friendly to strollers, river enthusiasts, and sunset watchers. It has proved to be one of the city's more successful revitalization efforts.

What further changes will Evansville see in the next 150 years? Will even the river keep rollin' along? No doubt whatever happens, The Evansville Courier will report it.